PUBLIC APOLOGY

(cor

I ..MHAIR.. are

my UNDYH FE /

SLIGHT sor... for the SELFISH /

IDIOTIC / INCONSIDERATE / ~~MILDLY~~

~~INCONVENIEN~~T thing/s I did

to MARTIN KELLIE and I solemnly

swear that I will ABSOLUTELY NEVER /

PROBABLY NEVER / SELDOM / ONLY ON

SPECIAL OCCASIONS repeat these actions.

Signed M.Shaw

Date 2.12.06

Other giftbooks in this series
Go Girl!
I Love You Madly
Little things mean a lot

Published simultaneously in 2005 by Helen Exley Giftbooks in Great Britain and Helen Exley Giftbooks LLC in the USA.

Illustrations © Caroline Gardner Publishing, Liz Smith and Helen Exley 2005
Text © Stuart and Linda Macfarlane 2005
Selection and arrangement copyright © Helen Exley 2005
The moral right of the author has been asserted.

ISBN 1-86187-759-5 | 12 11 10 9 8 7 6 5 4 3 2 1

Edited by Helen Exley
Pictures by Liz Smith and Caroline Gardner

Printed in China

Helen Exley Giftbooks, 16 Chalk Hill, Watford, Herts WD19 4BG, UK
Helen Exley Giftbooks LLC, 185 Main Street, Spencer MA 01562, USA
www.helenexleygiftbooks.com

Sorry

By Stuart & Linda
Macfarlane

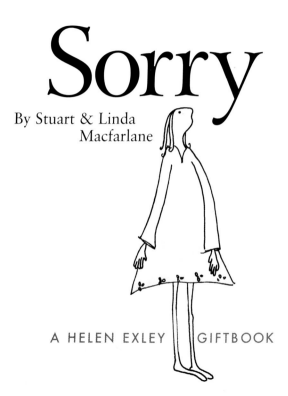

A HELEN EXLEY GIFTBOOK

I'M SORRY ...

I could shout the words
from the highest mountain
for all the world to hear.
I could paint the words across the moon
for all the world to see.
But – no matter how I say "I'm sorry",
it can never express the sorrow
I truly feel.

Being sor

worse than having toothache.

To say "sorry" I bought you
a single rose.
Next time I'll buy you two.

Until you forgive me
I won't eat, sleep, talk, smile,
or change my socks.
Everyone around me
hopes that you will forgive me.
Extremely soon.

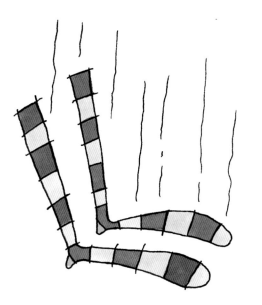

DIARY OF DISTRESS

Monday was awful
Tuesday was awful too
Wednesday was no better
Thursday was much worse
Friday I felt dreadful
Saturday was just grim
Sunday was worst of all.
Until you forgive me
Every day will be the same.

I intend writing you
the most magnificent poem....
I shall begin writing
as soon as I can think of a word
that rhymes with humiliated.

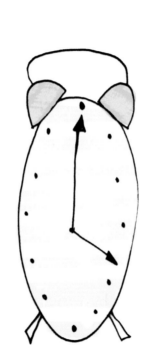

My world has ended,
The clock won't tick or tock,
There can be no bright tomorrow,
Chains of guilt my soul do lock.

For I have upset you,
But please hear my plea,
I beg your forgiveness,
Will you have mercy on me?

Please may I see you very soon.

I have something very important to say.

Meanwhile please practise

the following phrases:-

"Forget what you've done.
It's not important. I understand."

"Anyone could make such a mistake.
It doesn't matter."

"I forgive you completely.
Don't worry. Everything's fine."

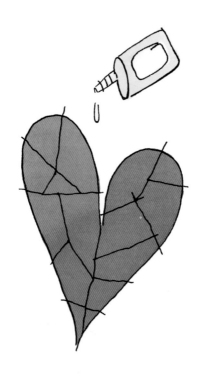

My heart it has been broken
  it's in a million bits
      but only you can mend it
and fix it so it fits.

Ninety thousand and forty two,
I'm sorry,
ninety thousand and forty three,
I'm sorry,
ninety thousand and forty four,
I'm sorry.
I'm saying sorry a gillion times
so you know exactly
how I feel....

If my tears were raindrops,
the world would be
completely flooded.
I am sorry for hurting you
and beg your forgiveness.

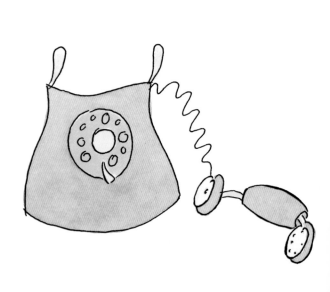

This is a recorded message....
I am too upset
to come to the phone.
I am lying in bed
and will stay here
until you forgive me
for everything
I have done wrong....
Please leave your message
of forgiveness after the tone....

My remorse is like a boomerang.
No matter how hard I try
to get rid of it,
it comes straight back
and thumps me on the head.

The leaves are tumbling
in my heart. Each one a symbol
of my remorse.

I would:

live to the depths of the deepest oceans
do battle with Neptune
wrestle with a Minotaur
hypnotise the giant Cyclops
shampoo Medusa's hair
ride Pegasus to the moon
all to gain forgiveness
from the most magical, mysterious,
magnificent creature ever – you.

This is a  genuine grov

beware of cheap imitations.

I've practised grovelling
and have become quite proficient.
I can grovel on my knees.
I can grovel on one leg.
can even grovel while standing on my head.
So, I beseech you please,
let me demonstrate my art
and maybe with all my grovelling
I can reach into your heart
and find forgiveness.

I wrote a list of over a million words

which express how bad I feel.

In order to save a few rain forests

here are just a few:-

Pathetic, deflated, unhappy, bewildered, mortified,

contrite, hopeless, dejected, desperate, remorseful,

disconsolate, distressed, embarrassed,

forlorn, gloomy, grim, guilty, heartbroken, humbled

dismal, humiliated, inconsolable, maudlin,

woeful, apologetic, miserable, penitent,

ghastly, regretful, despondent, downcast,

repentant, rueful.

My world fills with clouds

whenever I see

that I have made you sad.

To gain your forgiveness
I am willing to do *anything*.
Tick all those you wish me to perform:

- ❏ Praise you
- ❏ Remember your Birthday/Anniversary next year
- ❏ Buy you an expensive meal
- ❏ Grovel
- ❏ Hide under the bed
- ❏ Charm you
- ❏ Shave off all my body hair
- ❏ Admit you're intelligent
- ❏ Hug you
- ❏ Dazzle You
- ❏ Bring you three red roses

I bought a huge humble pie,
I wrapped it up in remorse,
I tied it with a ribbon
of repentance.
Open it up
and accept my massive apology.

A flower says "I like you",
"I need you", and "I'm sorry".
It also says,
"Forgive me quickly
for I'll wither away very soon".

Help!

Since upsetting you
I've noticed something odd.
I've got no shadow
and no reflection in the mirror.
What's more, I have a mass of hair
growing all over my body
and a huge bend in my neck.
Save my World!
The only way to stop me changing into
a vampire-dracula-banshee-werewolf
is for you to hug me and to say
everything is okay again.

Dear Majestic, Magnificent, Wonderful One, your humblest, weakest most pathetic subject begs to be allowed to enter your presence and eat the crumbs from your table, lick the dust from your shoes and strew rose petals before your every step. This would be heaven compared to the hell I am living without your smile.

There's no word in any dictionary
that can describe how awful I feel.
So I invented a word just for you –
"xqeiuatze".
I know, just like "sorry",
it's a difficult word to say
but it does sum up my feelings
quite perfectly.

I have the same bewildered,
devastated feeling
as the last dinosaur on Earth who,
looking around at the total annihilation
he had brought about,
had the final thought,
"So that's what that big switch marked
DO NOT PRESS
was for."

I'm feeling so utterly, abysmally sorry
that I bought you flowers.
They're wonderfully delicate, exquisite,
and fragrant.
In fact they're so nice
that if you don't forgive me immediately
I'm going to keep them for myself!

A BIG BIT OF SORROW

The Universe is bigger
Than any place it's true
But even it can't hold
The sorrow I feel for hurting you.

Forgive me
and put the sparkle
back in my life.

SORRY – It takes but 1 second
to say but ten million years
for me to recover
from the pain of hurting you.

Birds are too sad to sing
Dogs are howling in the streets
Cats have lost the will to sleep
Rabbits refuse to hop
Squirrels have gone into early hibernation.

Take pity on us poor creatures
While you remain angry at me
There can be no contentment
We are all tormented and distraught.

ONLY WORDS

I did not do what I meant to do,
didn't say the words I wanted.
'Cos if I did do what I meant to do
and had said the words I wanted,
then you would know what you
should know....
That I never would have done
such a silly thing in the first place.

Our friendship is like
a wonderful flower.
Through my stupidity
I have allowed it
to wilt and fade.
But with your forgiveness
it can blossom once more
into happiness.

I have bought
the biggest bottle of champagne
I could find.
I am humbly begging you
to forgive me
for all the silly things I have done.
Now, there is only one thing stopping us
from having
a fabulous celebration....

HERMIT

I've absolutely, definitely decided
I've really, truly made up my mind
To hide away for ever and ever
A hermit, a recluse – all alone.
Never, ever to be seen again.

I've packed up my bags
and I'm leaving.
Nothing could change my mind
Unless!!
You were to say "I forgive you"
In which case –
I'll be over in ten minutes.

A star dims
each time I think of the sadness
I have caused you.
Please forgive me
and let the stars shine again!

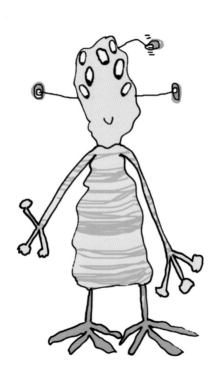

Would you believe me if I told you that
none of this was my fault.
That I was a billion miles away at the time.
That I was kidnapped by aliens and made slave
to a seven-eyed, orange jelly-creature
from another galaxy. That it was only
my undying admiration for you that gave me
the courage and strength to fight single handed
against their mighty armies then escape
on their spacecraft back to earth....

No?

Well, how about believing that I am truly, truly
sorry?

Helen Exley runs her own publishing company
which sells giftbooks in more than seventy countries.
Helen's books cover the many events and emotions in life,
and she was eager to produce a book to say a simple 'sorry'.
Caroline Gardner's delightfully quirky 'elfin' cards
provided the inspiration Helen needed to go ahead
with this idea, and from there this series of stylish
and witty books quickly grew:
Sorry, Go Girl!, I love you madly, and *Little things mean a lot.*

Caroline Gardner Publishing has been producing beautifully
designed stationery from offices overlooking the River Thames
in England since 1993 and has been developing the destinctive
'elfin' stationery range over the last five years.
There are also several new illustrations created especially for
these books by freelance artist and designer Liz Smith.

Stuart and Linda Macfarlane live in Glasgow, Scotland.
They have produced several books with Helen Exley
including *The Little Book of Stress, Old Wrecks' Jokes,*
and the hugely successful *Utterly adorable cats.*